T0361446

30 DAYS TO SELF-CONFIDENCE

sound
wisdom.
Because Your Success Matters

SOUND WISDOM BOOKS
BY EARL NIGHTINGALE

*Opportunities will not come
to you unless you have
an opinion of yourself big
enough to grasp them.*

—NAPOLEON HILL,
Self-Confidence Formula

EARL NIGHTINGALE

30 DAYS TO SELF-CONFIDENCE

A Guide to Stop Doubting Yourself
and Start Succeeding

THE STRANGEST SECRET SERIES

Published and distributed by:
SOUND WISDOM
P.O. Box 310
Shippensburg, PA 17257-0310
717-530-2122

info@soundwisdom.com

www.soundwisdom.com

ISBN 13 TP: 978-1-64095-507-3

ISBN 13 eBook: 978-1-64095-508-0

For Worldwide Distribution, Printed in the U.S.A.

1 2 3 4 5 6 7 8 / 28 27 26 25 24

*We become
what we think about.*

—EARL NIGHTINGALE

CONTENTS

INTRODUCTION

by Vic Conant

My dad, Lloyd Conant, met Earl Nightingale in 1956 when Earl was a popular radio commentator on WGN in Chicago. At the time, Dad was a successful businessman; he owned his own direct marketing and printing company. Earl had just produced a recording titled *The Strangest Secret* and was looking for someone to market that product. The two of them met, and Dad ended up selling a million of that recording over the years. These two men were a match made in Heaven: my dad the marketer and Earl the talent.

Earl, like Lloyd, was a Great Depression-era child and grew up poor in California. Earl educated himself; he was an avid reader and a brilliant guy. Both had only a high school education. Earl was a totally self-made man, as was my dad, so the two of them hit it off and eventually created Nightingale-Conant when I was about fourteen.

Every individual who has discovered what Earl Nightingale calls *The Strangest Secret* throughout the ages has found it to be a profoundly life-changing discovery. That secret? *You become what you think about*—and the fact that our thoughts *control* and—many believe—*create* our reality. Consequently, there is great responsibility placed on our thinking, making us responsible for our own future.

Vic Conant
Chairman of the Board
Nightingale-Conant Corporation

PERFECTLY NATURAL TENDENCIES

Each of us has a perfectly natural tendency to underestimate our own powers, to feel despair, to want more than anything else to quit. That's the time we should not quit.

In March 1956, an amazing thing happened to me. I was retiring from a very busy schedule and wanted to take it easy for a while. I decided to spend some time in Arizona. Since I'd be away, the manager of one of my small businesses asked if I would record a message he could play at the next sales meeting.

This made sense to me, so I decided to create a thirty-minute talk to encapsulate the important things I'd learned during my more than twenty years of research on why men and women succeeded or failed in life.

I spent quite a bit of time putting my thoughts and research together, and then I recorded the message and called it *The Strangest Secret*. Well, it wasn't long before people started asking for copies of the talk. And finally, we had to have it pressed into a record. At first, hoping that I might get back the cost of producing it—the masters, pressings, the record jacket, the artwork, the plates and all that—I arbitrarily set a price of $15. I figured that if it would help a person, it'd be worth $15, and if it didn't help, they could get their money back by returning it.

To my excitement, *The Strangest Secret* sold faster than I ever thought. I soon had back my original investment and so immediately dropped the price from $15 to $4.95, and then things really began to happen. My office had trouble keeping an adequate inventory. The record began to sell in the tens of thousands, and in a couple of years, we'd sold

It's an interesting reality about this business of living successfully. Once you know how, it's a whole lot easier than living unsuccessfully.

more than one hundred thousand copies to companies and individuals worldwide. I don't know whether you've ever had a bestseller on your hands or not, but I want to tell you it's just about the most interesting and exciting experience that can happen to a person.

What pleases me most, of course, has been the letters I've received telling me that what I shared had been helpful in some way in boosting their self-confidence and reliance. I spent so many years wallowing in confusion myself that I know what it is to get your life straightened out and on the right track for the first time.

It's an interesting reality about this business of living successfully. Once you know how, it's a whole lot easier than living unsuccessfully. All the confusion, running around in circles, the doubt and frustration disappear, and you can chart yourself a clear straight course to your goals in life and achieve each one with amazing regularity, one after another.

I know one thing for sure: 95 percent of the people who feel they're hemmed in and held down by circumstances can find they can achieve their goals right on schedule and get what they want out of life if they learn what I call *The Strangest Secret*. And anyone can learn it, even a child.

It has been said that people don't need education as much as they need reminding. I think most people really know what they should do to achieve what they want, but it's easy to forget what's important—especially if they lack self-confidence.

The greatest discovery of my generation is that human beings can alter their lives by altering their attitudes.

—WILLIAM JAMES

Self-Confidence Versus Self-Doubt Study Questions

1.   On a scale of 1 (low) to 10 (high), how would you rate your self-confidence?

2.   On the same scale, how would you rate your self-doubt?

3.   If you didn't rate self-confidence 10 and self-doubt 1, are you willing to take seriously the wisdom in this book to improve your outlook in life? To change attitudes that are holding you back from succeeding?

Notes:

_____

_____

_____

_____

_____

_____

_____

_____

_____

_____

_____

_____

GROWING OR DECAYING

Unless we throw ourselves into something challenging and interesting, we will begin to retrogress, to shrink, to die.

Have you ever wondered why some people keep growing even after they are what the world considers to be successful or have a successful business? Why does it keep growing long after reaching great success? One of our clients is a business firm that each year does several billion dollars worth of business. If I mentioned the name, it would be as familiar to you as your own.

The company was shooting for sales goals that would've appeared ridiculous a few years before. But now they were realistic goals and they would be reached. Still, you might wonder why. Why does a company doing billions of dollars worth of business, millions of dollars a month, keep setting higher goals? Why does it continue to expand and build and hire more people and get bigger?

We're as successful as we want to be.

Intelligent business people realize that a business is either growing or decaying. There's no such thing as standing still and surviving. You can never reach a place where you say, "This is it. We're as successful as we want to be. So now we'll just hold the fort and maintain our present volume and profit." No. There are too many variables. As Sir Isaac Newton proved in his laws of physics, a body in motion tends to remain in motion and a stationary body tends to remain stationary.

If a business or a person stood still and the rest of the country and the world's economy continued to advance, it would create a situation in which the business or the person would, inevitably go backward. If everything in the world stood still at the same time, it might be all right. But this is never the case. Our competition is not standing still.

Realizing this fact helps you understand that confidence in yourself, your business, your efforts, your everything brings reality. You may have great ideas and solutions, but without confidence, each will wither in your mind if not presented on paper and out loud to yourself and those who can help you achieve your goals.

Times are changing. Tastes and the likes and dislikes of the customer change, and we must change and grow with them or die. If a successful person considers themselves to be as successful as they want to be, collects all their marbles and quits, what then? What happens to a person's habits of hard work, of creative thinking and ability that they have devoted so many years to develop?

What happens to the enthusiasm for an exciting project? Unless we throw ourselves into something challenging and interesting, we will begin to retrogress, to shrink, to die. We can't stand still even if we want to, nor can anything in nature. A tree, any tree at any time, is either growing or decaying—and a business or person works the same way.

This is why the successful small business tends to grow into a successful large business. And successful large businesses tend to grow larger. It's good for everyone concerned: more jobs, more wealth, more productivity, more growth, and a higher standard of living for everyone. If you find yourself standing still, watch out.

Self-Confidence Versus Self-Doubt Study Questions

1. What products come to mind when you hear the phrase "new and improved"? What motivates people to keep creating and upgrading their businesses and/or products?

2. Likewise, what attributes and talents and skills come to mind when you hear the phrase "lifetime learner"?

3. Why is self-confidence a character quality you want to add to your personality? How will more confidence and less doubt bring about a "new and improved lifetime learner" in you? To what end?

Notes:

_____

_____

_____

_____

_____

_____

_____

_____

_____

_____

FOUR GROUPS

*Are you a productive, cost-conscious
and profit-minded person?*

J. Paul Getty, who amassed a personal fortune running into the billions of dollars, once wrote that people fall into four groups. While reading his perspective, see if you agree with him; and if you do, think about in which of the four categories you belong.

In the first group are those who work best when they work entirely for themselves. These are the entrepreneurs who are at their best when they own and operate their own businesses. They don't want to be employed by anyone. The security of a salaried job means nothing to them. They're willing to accept the risks involved in trusting their own directions and decisions.

In the second group you find those who do not wish to be in business for themselves, but who achieve excellent results when working for someone else and given the opportunity to share in the company's profits and growth.

Entrepreneurs are willing
to accept the risks involved
in trusting their own
directions and decisions.

These people are often commissioned salespeople who have no limit placed upon their earnings. They often advance to top executive positions. Mr. Getty cited the case of Charles Wilson, who went from an eighteen-cents-an-hour job to the $600,000-a-year presidency of General Motors. He was always an employee, but he made millions through the stock ownership of the companies he helped to build.

Number three in J. Paul Getty's list are those who enjoy the security of a steady salary and who don't like to take risks of any kind. These are fine, conscientious people and reliable workers with wonderful attendance records. They don't shoot for the top or even the near top, but are content with occasional raises of salary. They like to stay somewhere in the middle. They don't have the independence and initiative, nor perhaps the drive and self-confidence of the people in the first two groups. Perhaps they just don't care about moving up and are perfectly happy where they are.

And number four in this last group are those who simply don't care whether the company they work for shows a profit or a loss as long as they get their paychecks on time. Mr. Getty wrote that he's encountered specimens in this group, many of whom are graduates of leading schools of business administration, who can't even read a balance sheet and couldn't give an intelligent definition of what is meant by the words "prophets" versus "profits."

Group four feel little or no sense of responsibility to their employers nor to the stockholders of the company. They're interested only in their own personal welfare. They often try to reach the upper rungs of the success ladder and wonder why they never do. They don't seem to understand why they're never given the top jobs or make the top incomes. They're the ones who take the longest lunch hours and always leave right on the dot or even a little sooner to get home.

If a dollar was missing from their paycheck, they'd scream to high heaven, but they'll go to no trouble at all to save that dollar for the company they work for or think through moneymaking ideas for the good of the company. Strangely enough, this particular type of person has the wildest delusions of their own value , demands the most, and does the least.

To get a quick idea of your value to the economy, ask yourself if you're a productive, cost-conscious and profit-minded person. If so, you have what J. Paul Getty called the "millionaire mentality."

Self-Confidence Versus Self-Doubt Study Questions

1. Into which of the four groups do you fit? Is that the most beneficial, long-term group for you? Are you willing to make the move up into the first or second group?

2. How much more self-confidence would it take for you to consider making a move like that?

3. If you're a doubter, list your top five current doubts that are holding you back from taking any steps toward improving your lifestyle, career, or relationships.

Notes:

_____

_____

_____

_____

_____

_____

_____

_____

_____

_____

_____

CREATE A MILLIONAIRE MINDSET

Treat everyone you meet as the most important person on Earth.

Since our minds can hold only one thought at a time, make the thoughts you hold constructive and positive—not self-deprecating and doubtful. Look for the best in people and ideas—and yourself. Be constantly alert for new ideas you can put to use in your life. And don't waste time talking about your problems to people who can't solve them. It won't help.

Radiate the attitude of well-being and confidence—the attitude of someone who knows where they are going. When this is your attitude, all sorts of good things will happen to you.

And last, treat everyone with whom you come in contact as the most important person on Earth. Start this habit, practice it consistently, and it will benefit you for the rest of your life.

It's almost like a flirtation, the way some opportunities first grab your attention. Something new adds excitement. It may be a revolutionary idea that will bring you fame and fortune, or it could be just a get-rich-quick scheme and a limited future.

The test of our humanity is what we settle for.

The test of our humanity is what we settle for. One of the most interesting and irritating habits of human beings is their way of clinging to myths. A myth is defined as a traditional or legendary story that gets passed along from generation to generation—yet has *no* basis in fact. No matter how many times it's disproved, millions of people still believe untrue myths.

Have you ever heard the myth, "You can't change human nature"? I'll bet you've heard that a thousand times. People say there have to be wars because you can't change human nature, or people have to be poor because they came from a long line of poor people.

But the worst one of all, I suppose, is the one that goes, "Well, that's just the way things are, and there's nothing you can do about it." This one is especially harmful because of its general nature, its ambiguity. This is the myth that has clung to human beings for thousands of years—that circumstances decide what happens to us.

People, millions of them, strange as it seems, actually prevent themselves from getting a better, happier life by turning their backs on the reality of accepting the good in life and instead choosing to accept the gloom of disillusioning fiction.

Take, for example, the millions of men and women who spend year after year in a dismal, boring rut of existence. They don't like their lives, their jobs, their surroundings, or their places in the world—but they stay there. Rather than look into a few facts of life, they believe and accept the myth that they can't change circumstances. They believe that they are where they are, and for some reason they can't put their finger on, they have to stay there.

These people have all kinds of pet names for different aspects of circumstances like, "I could never get a break," "I never had a chance," "My folks didn't make me go to school," "I never had anything and I never will," or "I'm just not lucky like other people." I'm sure you've heard your share of these tales of woe. I have, and it's a shame the way some people let myths stand between them and a life of challenge, reward, and happiness. It's like they have built some misty, unreal wall between them and an enjoyable life.

And what causes all the trouble? These people listen to friends and relatives who don't know any more than they do.

Self-Confidence Versus Self-Doubt Study Questions

1. The first three paragraphs of Day 4 hold a multitude of good advice and dose of counsel regarding a lifetime of success! Which of the recommendations struck you as immediately doable? Which ones do you think would take some time to absorb into your lifestyle?

2. Do you have an "It is what it is" mindset? Why?

3. Are you ready to pursue a millionaire mindset? Or are you "doubtful"? What are your doubts based on? Myth or reality?

Notes:

_____

_____

_____

_____

_____

_____

_____

_____

_____

PUT YOUR MIND
TO USE

"Human nature...requires to grow and develop itself on all sides according to the tendency of the inward forces which make it a living thing."

On the other hand, there are wise people who have shared their wisdom for everyone to use to their advantage. For example, John Stewart Mill, who many identify as the most influential philosopher of the 19th century, wrote:

> He who lets the world, or his own portion of it, choose his plan of life for him has no need of any other faculty than the ape-like one of imitation. He who chooses his plan for himself employs all his faculties. He must use observation to see, reasoning and judgment to foresee, activity to gather materials for decision, discrimination to decide, and when he has decided, firmness and self-control to hold to his deliberate decision.

Human nature is not a machine to be built after a model and set to do exactly the work prescribed for it, but a tree, which requires to grow and develop itself on all sides according to the tendency of the inward forces which make it a living thing.

Now there's something you can believe, and it's no myth! Bad myths live because people want them to live, I guess. They want to lean on them, blame them for their troubles. People who want a myth to continue so they can have something other than themselves to blame will eventually wind up being stuck with it throughout their lives. *Let that not be you.*

People want a myth to continue so they can have something other than themselves to blame.

I offer you an idea for today that will double, triple, or even quadruple your present income. In fact, you can increase it as far as you want to. Be mindful of your thoughts. Our thoughts and what we choose to focus on are the main determinants in what comes our way. Consequently, everything you have is a result of how much you have put your mind to use.

If you've been an adult for any length of time, your annual income, the home you live in, the car you drive, every penny you spend and save is a result of the way in which you've used your thoughts and focus. Our thoughts determine our reality because they lead directly to our actions, and it is through our actions that we attain our goals. So if you think of yourself as a success and see the path forward, you will invest yourself wisely.

How often do you actually try to think of ways to make better use of your time, ability, and talents? These three fundamental personal resources represent your capital, and how you invest each of the three determines your return. Letting a day go by without trying to think of new and better ways of performing and producing is the same as throwing money away.

I remember hearing, as a kid, some well-meaning but uninformed character say, "Opportunity knocks only once, and you have to be ready when it appears, because it may never come again." This was a terrible thing for me to contemplate: *What if opportunity came by when I was asleep? What if it had already passed by before I learned it would only come once? What if I happened to be blinking my eyes or walking the other way at the time?*

Of course, later in life, I learned the truth. Opportunity doesn't come knocking at all. It simply exists. Opportunity is present all the time, every day, seven days a week—and our job is to recognize it and grab hold of it. Each day offers us the opportunity to indulge in the practice of thinking, which is the highest function of humans.

Self-Confidence Versus Self-Doubt Study Questions

1. Successful people "must use observation to see, reasoning and judgment to foresee, activity to gather materials for decision, discrimination to decide, and when he has decided, firmness and self-control to hold to his deliberate decision." Do you agree with this statement? Write it in your own words, reflecting your personal circumstances.

2. How often do you waste time thinking of your career mistakes, your failed relationships, or your lack of motivation? Now—how often do you productively use your time thinking of ways to make better use of your *time, ability,* and *talents*?

3. Are you taking advantage of every opportunity that presents itself every day? Do you daily practice *thinking,* which is the highest function of humans?

Notes:

_____

_____

_____

_____

_____

_____

DAY 6

JUST ONE
GOOD IDEA

*Just one good idea can revolutionize
your life for the better.*

If we don't avail ourselves of each opportunity to *think*, we simply pass it up. It's a chance lost, never to return, but it's great to know that it's never too late to begin. Ideas are free, and there are no limits. One good idea, just one, can revolutionize our lives for the better. One idea can double our rewards or increase them a thousandfold just as a single seed can eventually produce a forest.

Driving through a city in our cars, we see nothing but ideas in solid form—from people who were confident enough to step out and make a difference. Everything produced was first an idea in someone's mind—from the hotdog stand to the ballpark, from the tallest skyscraper to the city park, from the corner store to the giant corporate complex employing thousands. These are all ideas in tangible form.

If you find yourself uninterested in taking action about an idea, it's probably not the right idea for you. But when the right idea comes along, you will become so excited that you have to do something about it! When it comes, don't doubt and don't talk about it. That dissipates the excitement. *Do* something about it.

Use your focus to pursue your goals. The rewards will take care of themselves. They always do. That's the way a confident and self-assured mindset works.

There are no limits to ideas and opportunities, and there are no limits to the number of people who want to be successful.

If anyone thinks the glory days are over for inventors, and that all the good stuff has already been invented, just check the facts. In 1963, around 90,000 applications for patents were filed with the US Patent and Trademark office. In 2014, that number had increased to more than 615,000, over a half million new ideas worthy of a patent application in just one year. That's more than seventy every hour, twenty-four hours a day, or one just about every minute. There are no limits to ideas and opportunities, and there are no limits to the number of people who want to be successful.

That's a natural aspect of human nature. Step out and be part of it!

Self-Confidence Versus Self-Doubt Study Questions

1. While reading today's guide, did an idea come to mind? Even a faint suggestion of an idea? Maybe it wasn't a bridge to span the gap across two mountains, but rather a bridge to span the gap across a career change or across a widening relationship gap at work or at home?

2. Why do you think you were told not to tell anyone about your big idea?

3. Have you had a big idea, but doubt crept in, and you shoved it idea into a corner of your mind?

Notes:

_____

_____

_____

_____

_____

_____

_____

_____

_____

_____

SERVICE TO COMMUNITY

Successful people serve without fanfare through donations to charitable organizations.

It's perfectly natural for a person to want to be success-ful, but the majority of people in the United States are not successful people in any of the important categories that make a difference. What are these important categories? I'll name and number them:

1. **Recognition.** Successful people receive and give more recognition than unsuccessful people.

2. **Self-Esteem.** Self-esteem comes in part from recognition, but it also comes from the knowledge that we are in charge of our lives, and that we are proceeding along the planned route.

3. **Rewards.** The rewards of success come in many forms, not the least of which is in the form of money. Successful people earn more money than unsuccessful people and enjoy investing and

spending it. They live in better dwellings and drive better cars. They travel more, they meet more interesting people, and they have more options. Successful people don't have to spend the final years of their lives—which for successful people tend to be the best years—in limited or unfortunate circumstances. Successful people enjoy life more and tend to enjoy more years of life.

Successful people enjoy life more and tend to enjoy more years of life.

4. **Change.** The stimulation of change in our lives is of great importance. In fact, some experts in such matters believe change to be the second most important want on the part of people everywhere, right after recognition. As mentioned in category 3, successful people have much more stimulation and change in their lives. They can go more places, do more things, and meet more people. They're not stuck anywhere—physically, mentally, and relationally.

5. **Service.** Successful people do a better job of serving others than unsuccessful people, or they would not be successful. Their very success gives them more options and freedom to be of special service to others through foundations, libraries, hospitals, universities, the arts, and the like.

The self-confident, successful people of the country serve without fanfare through their donations to charitable organizations of all kinds. But the greatest service to the community by the successful of the world is through how their success was achieved. Whether an athletic star, performer, business person, or professional, their very success has served the community in one way or another.

To me, those are the five main categories through which successful people experience joy, satisfaction, and reward. The unsuccessful do not share in these experiences.

Self-Confidence Versus
Self-Doubt Study Questions

1.   How often do you recognize, appreciate, and acknowledge, either in person or in writing, the efforts of other people? Knowing this is an important category found in successful people, will you increase your recognitions?

2.   Self-esteem was the second important category. Look up the definitions for self-esteem and self-confidence. What are the differences? Similarities?

3.   How agreeable are you to change? Do you welcome changes such as a modification in work schedule, adjustment in a planned vacation, or a variation of a holiday tradition?

Notes:

_____

_____

_____

_____

_____

_____

_____

_____

UNSUCCESSFUL PEOPLE

*Unsuccessful people take their
cues in life from those around them,
which is a self-defeating cycle.*

When I think of unsuccessful people, I think of those men and women who are at the mercy of forces over which they seem incapable or uninterested in influencing. I was raised as a boy in challenging circumstances and came to know them well. During the Great Depression of the 1930s, I watched people who seemed helpless to do anything about their problems. Their most serious shortcoming was, of course, lack of education.

They took their cues from those around them, which is the self-defeating cycle of the poor. They follow the wrong group. The men and women with whom they talked and shared their misery had no more useful information than they themselves had and couldn't help them.

As I got older, about twelve, I began to ask people questions about our situation, and quickly discovered they knew no more than I did. They really didn't know anything at all, beyond existing in the most reactive way.

An unsuccessful person can usually be identified with an unsuccessful group.

If someone gave them a job, they worked. If someone didn't, they didn't work. There was no attempt of any sort at autonomy. They followed each other in waves or schools, as fish do. More than any other factor, perhaps, the unsuccessful person can usually be identified with a group.

The unsuccessful person is at the mercy of events because the unsuccessful person plays that part. "Que Sera, Sera, whatever will be will be," or it's God's will.

I say that the United States of America was built on the Protestant ethic that purports, "God helps those who help themselves." The successful person *does* things. The unsuccessful person has things done to or for them. The successful person seeks autonomy, makes their own plans, and has the self-esteem, inner excitement, and knowledge to know that those plans can be followed, barring a calamity.

Self-Confidence Versus Self-Doubt Study Questions

1. "When I think of unsuccessful people, I think of those men and women who seem to be at the mercy of forces over which they seem incapable or uninterested in influencing." In your point of view, is this an accurate definition? Why or why not?

2. The "self-defeating cycle of the poor" is the opposite of the self-confidence cycle of success. Explain why, and you will be on your way to stop doubting yourself and start succeeding!

3. Do you seek autonomy, make your own agenda, and have the self-confidence and inner excitement and knowledge to know that your plans—whatever they are—will succeed?

Notes:

_____

_____

_____

_____

_____

_____

_____

_____

POSITIVE INFORMATION FORMULATES IDEAS

When we present to our mind a problem to be solved, the mind goes to work to find the information we need to turn that idea into reality.

All information of a *positive* kind has value when we're formulating ideas. Information of a *negative* kind—self-doubt, low self-esteem, no confidence—has the opposite effect.

When we set an important goal for ourselves, we present to our mind a problem to be solved, a challenge to be successfully fulfilled. Instantly, far down in the labyrinth of its vast potential, the mind goes to work to find the information we need to turn that idea into reality.

For example, the idea of owning an automobile becomes an actual automobile we can drive and wash on a warm Sunday afternoon. Perhaps our path from inception of the idea to the time we get into the vehicle, turn the key, and drive away is rather torturous, even circular, leading first here and then there. But when we resolve to make it happen and don't give up—there it is in the driveway.

Ultimately, the idea has become real in our life.

More often than not, though, we get in our own way by doubting the suggestions that filter into our consciousness. But eventually, the idea, the invisible idea, becomes sheet metal and glass and upholstery and rubber—and from time to time a pain in the neck as well. Ultimately, the idea has become real in our life, even if it takes several years to pay for it.

Everything we obtain during our lifetimes comes to us as a result of that system. Often, it consists of nothing more than a trip to the grocery store or a telephone call or a command to a teenager, followed by the rationalization of the command and perhaps the additional idea of offering some sort of reward for following through on the idea.

Self-Confidence Versus Self-Doubt Study Questions

1. Do you routinely feed your mind with positive or negative thoughts and imaginations? What are the results when you're filled with positivity? Negativity?

2. What is a recent idea that you doubted and didn't take action on, causing it to eventually whither and die? Is it time to resurrect it?

3. What is a recent idea that you followed through with action and commitment, causing it to become a reality? Did that boost your self-confidence?

Notes:

_____

_____

_____

_____

_____

_____

_____

_____

_____

_____

IDEAS FOLLOWED BY FULFILLMENT

We are responsible for the choices we make from the spectrum of options we confront and how our education prepares us.

Ideas are followed by fulfillment. As our ideas progress upward in degree, cost, and complication, we still follow the same process that results in fulfillment or being frightened off by timidity, rationalization, or, on occasion, just plain good common sense. Sometimes, as we toy or tinker with a delicious idea, our thinking process is flooded by other ideas, indicating that particular delicious idea will have to be postponed for a year or two or maybe even more.

Our thinking process tells us we've made the kind of quantum leap that's out of place if we were to stick to our present hierarchy of plans and ideas. That's why a written list is a good idea. We can also modify that list from time to time. In fact, as we learn how readily such a system brings us fulfillment of our goals, it's not at all unusual to upgrade our list to include levels we may not at first had thought were in the ballpark for us. Millions of people use this process without giving it a second thought, without understanding the process at all.

A system once understood and tested can be applied to whatever we consider gold material. All we need to do is leave it to the system. We don't have to fully understand the system in order to use it. The more we try to rationalize and understand every aspect of the working process, the more we tend to get in our own way and limit our potential. It works. Leave it at that.

The choices we prepare for and make lead us to the life we will have and who we will become. Each person is responsible for what we become by virtue of the choices we make from the great spectrum of options we confront and how our education prepares us. Our rich genetic inheritance gives each of us a wide range of options, and our free society gives us free choice from that range of options.

The more we try to rationalize and understand every aspect of the idea fulfillment process, the more we tend to get in our own way and limit our potential.

Self-Confidence Versus Self-Doubt Study Questions

1. The choices we prepare for and make lead us to the life we will have and who we will become. Are you preparing for success by becoming more self-confident? Do you naturally live with a millionaire mindset and expect certain results?

2. You are responsible for what you become by virtue of the choices you make from the great spectrum of options you confront and how your education prepares you. Have you educated yourself in areas that lead to your success?

3. "Our rich genetic inheritance gives each of us a wide range of options and our free society gives us free choice from that range of options." In your mind, is this an true statement? If you don't agree, consider that may be why you lack self-confidence and are doubtful. Take that statement as truth, making it personal, and memorize it to give you the boost you need to believe it and live it! "My rich genetic inheritance gives me a wide range of options and my free society gives me free choice from that range of options."

Notes:

_____
_____
_____
_____
_____
_____
_____
_____
_____
_____
_____
_____
_____
_____
_____
_____
_____
_____
_____
_____
_____
_____
_____
_____
_____

_____

_____

_____

_____

_____

_____

_____

_____

_____

_____

_____

_____

_____

_____

_____

_____

_____

_____

_____

_____

_____

_____

A GREAT SPECTRUM OF OPTIONS

Every new idea raises a curtain on a new window of possible interest and opportunity.

The better the environment in which we're raised or the better our education as young people and the better the education of our parents, the greater the spectrum of options we will be exposed to during our formative years. Each new idea we're exposed to raises a curtain on a new window of possible interest and opportunity.

For example, a child raised in a small village deep in the hills of an isolated area may seem to be at the minimum range of options exposure, but books and the internet can bring to the child a whole world beyond that valley. Therefore, there are only a few places in our country where a youngster doesn't have access to a great spectrum of options.

When we fully understand that we *become what we think about,* we begin to see how our goals can lead us to whatever requirements are necessary. The youngster who dreams of becoming, a physician knows that college and medical school are necessary. We become what we think about all the years of our lives, and we can easily tell the extent and quality of a person's thinking by simply observing the magnitude and quality of that person's life.

When we fully understand that we become what we think about, we see how our goals lead us to whatever is necessary.

Self-Confidence Versus Self-Doubt Study Questions

1. How great is your spectrum of options based on your childhood environment, your education, and the education of your parents—whether formal or self-taught?

2. Because each new idea we're exposed to raises a curtain on a new window of possible interest and opportunity, how wide open is your window? How many interests and opportunities are within reach?

3. Because it's true that you become what you think about throughout your life, what would those close to you say about the magnitude and quality of your life right now?

Notes:

_____

_____

_____

_____

_____

_____

_____

_____

_____

_____

_____

_____

_____

_____

_____

_____

_____

_____

_____

_____

_____

_____

_____

_____

_____

_____

_____

_____

_____

_____

_____

WHAT DO YOU BELIEVE?

Let me ask you a rather personal question. What do you believe in?

It sometimes seems that people are experiencing so much doubt, fear, and cynicism—so much tongue-in-cheek and wise-guy-elbow-rib-poking—that we've come to the place where people don't believe in anything anymore. As doubt creeps in, self-confidence creeps out, and people waver making even the most simple decisions.

So what do you believe in? This is an important question. It's vital that each of us decides exactly what we believe in. And I'll tell you why—because what you believe in determines the course of your life, what happens to you, and your ultimate destiny.

The great truth, "As you believe, so shall it be done unto you," seems to go almost unnoticed today, but that's exactly the way life works. What you believe in is what will happen to you. For belief is faith, and faith is still the greatest power on Earth.

What you believe in determines the course of your life, what happens to you, and your ultimate destiny.

A young medical student was being examined by a board of distinguished doctors to determine whether or not he would receive his license to practice. The student was asked, "Why do you want to be a physician?"

He replied, "I've known I was going to be a doctor for as long as I can remember. There's simply no question about it. I'm going to be a practicing physician and a good one." He told them he was going to be a doctor. They had no choice in the matter.

What we believe makes us who we are. The greater our faith, the greater we become.

Self-Confidence Versus Self-Doubt Study Questions

1. Are you experiencing doubt, fear, and cynicism?
    Have you been the brunt of sly or cruel jokes
    that make you doubt your judgment of what's
    right or wrong? Do you voice your opinions
    with boldness or meekness or not at all?

2. What you believe in is what will happen to you. Do you
    believe in yourself, that you are a unique gift to the
    world? Do you believe that you can be successful?
    Do you believe that you are here on Earth for a great
    purpose? These statements are true. Believe.

3. Can you choose to believe that the best will
    prevail? That good will overcome anything
    otherwise? Can you say confidently, as did the
    young medical student, "I've known I was going to
    be a _____ for as long as I can
    remember. There's simply no question about it. I'm
    going to be a _____ and a good one."

Notes:

_____

_____

_____

_____

DAY 13

FAITH?
OR WANTING
AND WISHING?

*What would you be willing to risk because
of the certainty of your belief?*

The difference between faith and wanting or wishing is
that with faith, we know what's going to be. By wanting or
wishing, we're only hoping. It's what we believe that makes
us the kind of people we are. The greater our faith, the
greater we become.

People who let others do their thinking for them, who
will not offer an opinion on any subject until they're sure
that what they say will be met with approval and acceptance, do not believe. They conform to what they think
others want them to be like. They are chameleons ready
to take on any hue their surroundings demand. They have
no deep anchors of belief and so drift aimlessly on the
surface of life.

*The greater your faith,
the greater you become.*

So when I asked you, "What do you believe in?" I meant, what do you have faith in? Would you be willing to risk everything you have on the certainty of your belief?

If a person believes he or she isn't much of a person, that's what they will be. If they believe they have value, that no one on Earth is exactly like them, that they have an important contribution to make, and that they can reach their goals, these beliefs will all be true and will come to pass.

People remain where they are because they believe that's where they ought to be—contrarywise, people rise to new heights of achievement and ability because they believe they will. The greatest teachers who ever lived—people whose minds soared far above those of their times and whom we still read and believe—said that according to our faith will it be done unto us.

And that, my friend, is the way it works. There are no arguments, no exceptions, no hair-splitting. Not only is it the way to build self-confidence, it's a perfectly natural tendency—*what you believe is who you become.*

Self-Confidence Versus Self-Doubt Study Questions

1. Do you allow others to think for you? Do you need others' approval and acceptance before you offer an opinion? If so, you are conforming rather than believing. Do certain recent situations come to mind when reading these questions? Are you prepared to change your mindset from conformation to self-directed, autonomous thinking?

2. Do you believe you have value, that no one on Earth is exactly like you, that you have an important contribution to make, and that you can reach your goals? These beliefs will all be true and will come to pass—when you believe. Do you?

3. "People remain where they are because they believe that's where they ought to be—contrarywise, people rise to new heights of achievement and ability because they believe they will." Which group of people are you more in tune with?

Notes:

_____

_____

_____

_____

COMPETENT THINKING

*Becoming competent is the first
step in competent thinking, and that
step starts for most in school.*

So often, youngsters in school worry about a passing grade. Freshmen in high school and college are frequently plagued by doubts as to whether or not they can successfully complete the four years ahead and graduate. Four years seem like such a long time to them, almost forever. And this thought sometimes leads to a sort of giving up, a fear of failure.

Harvard teacher and psychologist William James said in effect, "Let not students worry about the success of their efforts. If they will do each day as best they can, the work which is before them, they will wake up one day to find themselves among the competent people of their generation."

Students, executive homemakers, laborers, senior executives, and professionals—James's comments work for everybody. They remove doubt, fear, and worry, and bring order into our lives. All any of us needs to do is confidently face each day as it comes in good cheer, knowing that we have only to succeed today to guarantee our future.

In this way, we'll move steadily ahead, growing more competent, more confident with the passing of every day. Others may seem to suddenly shoot up faster and possibly fall much further. They may operate in spurts and fits, but it's to the steady that the rewards are eventually paid. Saint Edmond of Canterbury was right when he said, *"Work as though you would live forever, but live as though you would die tomorrow."*

Face each day as it comes in good cheer, knowing that we have only to succeed today to guarantee our future.

Self-Confidence Versus Self-Doubt Study Questions

1. Sometimes, the future holds long-term efforts to bring accomplishment. Sometimes, it seems almost like forever. Does this thought sometimes lead you to want to give up because of a fear of failure?

2. "If they will do each day as best they can, the work which is before them, they will wake up one day to find themselves among the competent people of their generation." In every endeavor, do you do the best you can the work before you? Do you remember a day when you "woke up" realizing that your best reaped you success? That "morning" can happen repeatedly when you confidently do your best daily.

3. When you move steadily ahead, growing more competent, more confident every day, rewards are eventually paid in full. Are you steadily moving ahead?

Notes:

_____

_____

_____

_____

_____

_____

FINISH WHAT YOU START

There's nothing mysterious about achieving outstanding success—it is completely within our individual control and absolutely predictable.

Write down the six most important things you have to do tomorrow. Then number them in the order of their importance. I encourage you to really do this. First thing tomorrow morning, tackle number one and stay with it till it's completed. If something should force its delay, move on to number two, but take them in order and finish them in order as best you can. Try not to get sidetracked by people or things as you successfully accomplish each task of your day.

Beside my typewriter, I have glued to the wall a great saying by Ernest Hemingway. He said, *"Write as well as you can and finish what you start."* There's nothing mysterious or capricious about achieving outstanding success. It's completely within our individual control and is absolutely predictable. It's simply a matter of doing certain things a certain way every day, and that's all there is to it. As long as you've got that goal to work toward, there's no reason on Earth why you should not become really successful in your field, your home life, and your community.

Remember that everything in the entire limitless universe operates on the law of cause and effect. There are no exceptions to this. Nothing happens by accident. For every result, there's a cause. You have only to take care of the cause. The effect will always, without exception, take care of itself. Good cause, good effect, no cause, no effect, bad cause, bad effect. It's as reliable as the rising of the sun.

Success is simply a matter of doing certain things a certain way every day.

Self-Confidence Versus
Self-Doubt Study Questions

1. If you haven't already, write down the six most important things you have to do tomorrow. Then number them in the order of their importance. Really do this. Now.

2. First thing tomorrow morning, tackle number one, and stay with it till it's completed. If something should force its delay, move on to number two, but take them in order and finish them in order as best you can.

3. Do not get sidetracked. If you have your goal to work toward each and every day, there's no reason why you should not become successful in your field, your home life, and your community.

4. Repeat steps 1, 2, and 3 daily!

Notes:

_____

_____

_____

_____

_____

_____

_____

ONE DAY AT A TIME

Living one day at a time the best we can, has an almost unbelievable cumulative effect for good, for success, and the things we want.

This business of living one day at a time the best we can has an almost unbelievable cumulative effect for good, for success and the things we want. Sometimes, when we see a bricklayer starting on a building and putting the first brick in place, we're struck by the size of the job he has ahead of him. But one day, almost before we realize it, he's finished. All the thousands of bricks are in place. Each one vital to the finished structure, each one sharing its portion of the load. And so should be the days of a human life if we want to be proud and happy with the finished product.

Now, let's consider one hundred men who start at the age of twenty-five believing that they will be successful. At twenty-five, if you ask any one of these men if he wants to be a success, he'll tell you he does. And you notice that he is eager toward life, there is a certain sparkle in his eye, an erectness to the way he carries himself. Life seems like a pretty interesting adventure to him.

But by the time those hundred men are age sixty-five, one will be rich, four will be financially independent, five will still be working, and fifty-four will be broke. Now think a moment: out of one hundred men, only five will actually be successful. Why do so many fail? What has happened to the sparkle that was there when they were twenty-five? What becomes of the dreams, the hopes, the plans? And why is there such a large disparity between what these men intended to do and what they actually accomplished?

When we say about five percent achieved success, we have to define success. And here's the best definition I've ever been able to find: Success is the progressive

Success is the progressive realization of a worthy ideal.

realization of a worthy ideal. If a man is working toward a predetermined goal and knows where he's going, that man is a success. If he's not doing that, he's a failure.

Rollo May, the distinguished psychiatrist, wrote a wonderful book, *Man's Search for Himself.* In this book he says, "The opposite of courage in our society is not cowardice. It is conformity." And there you have the trouble today— conformity rather than self-confidence. People act like everyone else without knowing why, without knowing where they're going.

Now think of it. In the United States of America, as of 2021, there were more than 55 million people sixty-five years of age and older, and many are living in poverty. They're dependent on someone else or the government for life's necessities.

Self-Confidence Versus
Self-Doubt Study Questions

1. Are you living each day the best you can?
    Truthfully, are you giving one hundred
    percent? Fifty percent? Twenty percent?

2. If "success is the progressive realization of a
    worthy ideal," define your "worthy ideal" and
    how you are progressively going to realize it.

3. Have you been known to conform to what others
    are doing at work, school, church, or at home? Or
    are you known as a non-conformist who makes your
    own way in life, sometimess "bucking the system"?

Notes:

_____

_____

_____

_____

_____

_____

_____

_____

_____

_____

DAY 17

TO CONFORM OR
NOT TO CONFORM

*Why do people with goals succeed in
life, and those without goals fail?*

Most children learn to read by the time they are seven years old, and most adults learn to make a living by the time they are twenty-five. Usually, by that time, not only are they making a living, many are supporting a family. And yet, by the time the majority are sixty-five, they haven't learned how to become financially independent in the richest land that has ever been known.

Why? We conform. We act like the ninety-five out of a hundred who don't succeed.

Why do most people conform? Well, they really don't know. These people believe that their lives are shaped by circumstances, by things that happen to them, by exterior forces. They're outer-directed people. A survey was made of working men who were asked, "Why do you work? Why

Unsuccessful people's lives are shaped by circumstances and exterior forces.

do you get up in the morning?" Outrageously, nineteen out of twenty had no idea, saying something like, "Well, everyone goes to work in the morning." And that's the reason they do it—because everyone else is doing it.

Self-Confidence Versus Self-Doubt Study Questions

1. Do you know why you do what you do? Most of the time, are you a follower or a leader?

2. Have your big decisions been made by thinking, contemplating, researching, and considering all the possibilities? Or have your big decisions been made by asking others, taking the easiest way out, and following other people's route in life?

3. What would you do and what lengths would you go if you knew your life could be free from doubt and fear?

Notes:

_____

_____

_____

_____

_____

_____

_____

_____

_____

_____

_____

_____

_____

_____

_____

_____

_____

_____

_____

_____

_____

_____

_____

_____

_____

_____

_____

_____

_____

BELIEVE AND SUCCEED

You become what you think about.

Here is the key to success and the key to failure—we become what we think about. Now read that simple yet very important statement again and make it personal: *I will become what I think about.*

Throughout history, teachers, philosophers and prophets have disagreed with one another on many different things. It's only on this one point that they're in complete and unanimous agreement—people become what they think about.

Marcus Aurelius, a great Roman emperor, said, "A man's life is what his thoughts make of it." Disraeli said, "Everything comes if a man will only wait. I've brought myself by long meditation to the conviction that a human being with a settled purpose must accomplish it and that nothing can resist a will that will stake even existence for its fulfillment." Ralph Waldo Emerson said, "A man is what he thinks about all day long."

William James (known as the father of American psychology) said, "The greatest discovery of my generation is that human beings can alter their lives by altering their attitudes of mind." He also said: "We need only in cold blood act as if the thing in question were real. And it will become infallibly real by growing into such a connection with our life that it will become real. It will become so knit with habit and emotion that our interest in it will be those which characterize belief." He also said:

> If you only care enough for a result, you'll almost certainly attain it. If you wish to be rich, you will be rich. If you wish to be learned, you will be learned. If you wish to be good, you'll be good. Only you must then really wish these

"We need only in cold blood act as if the thing in question were real."

things and wish them exclusively and not wish at the same time a hundred other incompatible things just as strongly.

The great law, briefly and simply stated, is that if you think in negative terms, you will get negative results. If you think in positive terms, you will achieve positive results. That is the simple fact, which is the basis of an astonishing law of prosperity and success: *believe and succeed.* William Shakespeare put it this way, "Our doubts are traitors and make us lose the good we often might win by fearing to attempt."

Self-Confidence Versus Self-Doubt Study Questions

1. Of the four men quoted, which quote resonated with you most? Write it in your own words. Are you serious enough to put it into practice as your life philosophy?

2. Can success be as simple as "believe and succeed"?

3. Tomorrow morning, I challenge you to guess how many negative thoughts you will have during the day and how many positive thoughts. Then keep a running count of each. Do you think you can guess the right number? You may be very surprised!

Notes:

_____

_____

_____

_____

_____

_____

_____

_____

_____

_____

THOUGHTS

*Those who think about nothing,
become nothing.*

George Bernard Shaw said, "People are always blaming their circumstances for what they are. I don't believe in circumstances. The people who get on in this world are the people who get up and look for the circumstances they want, and if they can't find them, make them." Well, that's pretty apparent, isn't it? And every person who discovered this truth for a while believed that he was the first one to figure it out.

If we become what we think about, it stands to reason that a person who thinks about a concrete and worthwhile goal is going to reach it. Conversely, the person who has no goal, who doesn't know where he's going—his thoughts will be of confusion and anxiety and fear and worry. His life becomes one of frustration and fear and anxiety and worry. And those who think about nothing become nothing.

The successful person says, "I'm going to become this," then works toward that goal.

Now let's go back to our definition of success. Who succeeds? The only person who succeeds is the person who is progressively realizing a worthy ideal. The self-confident, successful person says, "I'm going to become this," and then begins to work toward that goal.

A successful person is the school teacher who's teaching school because that's what they want to do. The successful person is the woman who's a wife and mother because she wanted to become a wife and mother and is doing a good job of it. The successful person is the man who runs the corner gas station because that was his dream. That's what he wanted to do. The successful person is the salesperson who wants to become a top-notch seller and grow and build the business.

Self-Confidence Versus Self-Doubt Study Questions

1. Have you realized that you are not held down or held back because of your circumstances? Are you ready to look for the circumstances you want, and if you can't find them, you'll make them?

2. Are your thoughts full of confusion, anxiety, or worry? What can you do to change those thoughts into a clear, purposeful, and excitedly happy chain of ideas and feelings?

3. What is your definition of success—what do you want? What is your goal?

Notes:

_____

_____

_____

_____

_____

_____

_____

_____

_____

_____

SPARKY'S STORY

What can happen to a loser?

A success is anyone who is doing a job they decided to do, and enjoying it, but only one out of twenty of us does that. That's why today, there isn't really any competition unless we make it for ourselves. Instead of competing, all we have to do is create.

This is the story about what can happen to a loser. When he was a little boy, the other kids called him "Sparky" after a comic strip horse named Spark Plug. Sparky never did shake that nickname. School was all but impossible for Sparky. He failed every subject in the eighth grade—every subject. He flunked physics in high school and received a flat zero for the course. He distinguished himself as the worst physics student in his school's history. He also flunked Latin and Algebra and English. He didn't do much better in sports. Although he did manage to make the school's golf team, he promptly lost the only important match of the year. There was a consolation match, however, and Sparky lost that, too.

Throughout his youth, Sparky was socially awkward. He was not actually disliked by the other youngsters; no one cared that much. He was astonished if a classmate ever said hello to him outside school hours. No way to tell how he might've done at dating because, in high school, Sparky never once asked a girl out. He was too afraid of being turned down. Sparky was a loser. Everyone knew it, so he rolled with it.

Sparky made up his mind early in life that if things were meant to work out, they would; otherwise, he would content himself with what appeared to be his inevitable mediocrity. But there was one thing that was important

Deliberately deciding your future—how a chronic underachiever can become famous worldwide.

to Sparky: drawing. He was proud of his own artwork. Of course, no one else appreciated it. In his senior year of high school, he submitted some cartoons to the editors of his class yearbook. Almost predictably, they were rejected. Despite this particularly painful rejection, Sparky was so convinced of his artistic ability that he decided to become a professional artist.

Upon graduating from high school, he wrote a letter to Walt Disney Studios. He was told to send some samples of his artwork, and the subject matter for a cartoon was suggested. Sparky drew the proposed cartoon. He spent a great deal of time on it and the other drawings. Finally, the reply from Disney Studios came. He was rejected once again, another loss for the loser.

So Sparky wrote his own autobiography in cartoons. He described his childhood self—the little boy loser, the chronic underachiever—in a cartoon character that was soon to become famous worldwide. For the boy who failed every subject in the eighth grade and whose work was rejected again and again was "Sparky" Charles Schultz! He created the Peanuts comic strip and the little cartoon boy whose kite would never fly, Charlie Brown.

Self-Confidence Versus Self-Doubt Study Questions

1. A success is anyone who is doing a job they decided to do, and enjoying it, but only one out of twenty of us does that. Are you that one out of twenty?

2. Would you have Charles Schultz's stamina to keep pushing ahead after so many rejections over so many years? Is there such a thing as too many rejections?

3. Do you ever feel like a loser? In what ways did Charles Schultz's story give you hope and the fortitude to press on?

Notes:

_____

_____

_____

_____

_____

_____

_____

_____

TWO KINDS OF PROBLEMS

About ninety-five percent or more of our problems are within our own personal power to solve.

Even if you were not a very good student, there may be a great entrepreneurial adventure in your future. Lots of people at the top were not good students, but they made it. What did they know?

It's not necessary for an individual to have technical training in the field of psychology to understand and appreciate the unlimited creative power of the human mind. Of course, the more knowledge, the better, but let me give you an example of how you can put your subconscious to work. First, pick a problem you want very much to solve. It can be anything: increasing your income, solving a business problem, writing a story, or solving a personal problem of some kind. Any kind of problem.

Realize right at the outset that there are two kinds of problems: 1) those over which we can exercise no control and 2) those we as individuals can solve. If you fall out of a tree, the problem is then out of your hands, but about ninety-five percent or more of our problems are within our own personal power to solve.

Second, state the problem, write it out in complete and simple detail, realize that it can be solved, and begin to turn it over in your mind.

Think of as many possible solutions as possible. Realize that you're merely feeling it out, starting your subconscious to work, and that the likelihood of your solving it with your conscious mind is pretty slim. Read and study as much as possible pertaining to your problem, and then forget it. Think of something else. Try not to think consciously of the problem at all.

If nothing happens for twenty-four hours or so, do it all over again. Attack the problem with your conscious mind, work on it as hard as you can, and then forget it again. One fine day soon, you'll be relaxing, thinking of nothing at all, and the solution will come perfectly clear and logical. Trying to solve problems with a conscious mind only is limiting yourself.

About
ninety-five percent or
more of our problems
are within our
own personal power
to solve.

Self-Confidence Versus Self-Doubt Study Questions

1. Are you a natural problem-solver? Many people see problems and immediately want to solve them—usually for other people. How good are you at solving your own problems?

2. Are you facing a problem right now that seems impossible to solve? Will you take the author's advice to research and read about the issue, then forget about it for a while?

3. How convinced are you that your subconscious mind is capable of solving what your conscious mind can't always solve?

Notes:

_____

_____

_____

_____

_____

_____

_____

_____

_____

THE WORLD WITHIN

*To develop your full problem-solving abilities, learn to use the creative power of your subconscious **and** your conscious, continuously and intelligently.*

You can use all of your mental ability by stating the problem consciously and then letting your subconscious do the work for you. Every experience or condition of our life, success or failure, progress or frustration, growth or stagnation, is a result of an action or process selected and set in motion by our conscious mind. But to develop our full powers, it is necessary that we learn to use the creative power of both functions of our mind, the subconscious as well as the conscious, continuously and intelligently.

Every condition, every experience of life, is the result of our mental and emotional activity. We can do only what we think we can do. We can have only what we think we can have. Everything we do and have is the result of thought. We never express anything that we do not first have in our mind. Hence, the secret of attainment, progress, and developing a creative personality is found in constructive mental and emotional activity.

The external world is only a reflection of the world within us. Whatever is imagined in our inner life will be reflected in our personal world. Our mental and emotional activity focused on a desire, a picture in our mind, will supply us with limitless energy and will take whatever form our mind demands. Thoughts of personal growth and progress, of earning a good income, having influence with people, and experiencing satisfaction in daily life will become our reality. Your reality!

What we call success and happiness reflect themselves in time in the conditions under which we work and live. Thoughts of doubt, frustration, failure, and personal limitations operate in precisely the same fashion. When the average person is told that their mind has unlimited power available for their use, the statement is usually passed off as high-pressure inspiration. Yet, the facts of everyday experience prove that the human mind actually has amazing powers that few of us ever draw upon.

The secret to progress and developing a creative personality is in constructive mental and emotional activity.

Self-Confidence Versus Self-Doubt Study Questions

1. Developing a creative personality to boost self-confidence requires constructive mental and emotional activity. Can you list several constructive (productive) and emotional (positivity) activities that are part of your current personality?

2. Your mental and emotional activity focused on a wholesome desire supplies you with limitless energy. What does "limitless energy" mean to you? How would that energy enhance your life and lifestyle?

3. Do you believe that your mind has extraordinary powers to solve your problems, improve your everyday life, and bring success to every aspect of your world, including work, relationships, and health?

Notes:

_____

_____

_____

_____

_____

_____

_____

_____

DAY 22

DRIFTING

*Your subconscious mind seemingly has
unlimited power and strength available
in times of emergency and danger.*

So slight is our knowledge and so limited is our faith. The easiest thing in the world is to drift without purpose or direction. But when we do this, we're letting the creative power of our mind go to waste.

Modern science is based on controlled experimentation and observation, and the only way any person can know whether or not their mind really does have unlimited power available is to test the idea with personal experience.

Realize that your great subconscious mind must act on orders given by your conscious mind; so, give it a job to do and then watch the results. Then give it a bigger job, and then another. Top business executives and leaders in the field of science realize how this works and use this technique to solve their problems and reach their goals. You can do the same.

There lurks deep within you a wellspring of talent, even genius.

It has been written that there lurks deep within each of us a wellspring of talent, even genius. If it is to be found, it will come through the systematic exploration of our subconscious minds. What gives to a single woman the strength to lift a car when her child is trapped beneath it? From what source is the soldier in battle inspired and empowered to perform amazing acts of heroism and daring? What gives men and women the strength during earthquakes and fires to perform deeds utterly impossible under normal conditions?

According to many, it's through the subconscious mind that seemingly unlimited power and strength are available in such times of emergency and danger.

Self-Confidence Versus
Self-Doubt Study Questions

1. Is it easy for you to drift through a day, weekend, or week without purpose or direction, letting the creative power of your mind go to waste?

2. Your great subconscious mind acts on orders from your conscious mind; so, use this technique to solve your problems and reach your goals for success. With each achievement, your self-confidence will soar! Do you believe this?

3. Have you heard or, or even seen, impossible feats done by average people during times of stress or danger? It was reported on *CNN* and in *The Washington Post* in 2019 that a sixteen-year-old rushed next door after hearing cries for help. The neighbor was pinned underneath his car, and the teen quickly lifted the front of the car just high and long enough for his mother and the neighbor's wife to roll the man out from underneath.[1,2] Amazing, right?

---

1. Jacob Bogage, "High School Football Player Lifts Car Off Neighbor's Chest Hailed Hero," *The Washington Post,* September 27, 2019; https://www.washingtonpost.com/sports/2019/09/27/high-school-football-player-lifts-car-off-neighbors-chest-hailed-hero/; accessed January 12, 2024.

2. For other amazing acts of selfless heroism that will encourage you and boost your self-confidence, visit https://www.wearethemighty.com/articles/heroes-9-11/; accessed January 15, 2024. Paul Szoldra, "7 incredible stories of heroism on 9/11," *History, We Are The Mighty,* September 10, 2019.

SUPERHUMAN STRENGTH

In the presence of danger, superhuman strength is available, a vast reserve of power in the unexplored field of subconscious motivation.

Now, consider this case. The late Dr. Brown Landone[3] was one of the really great men of a past generation. He was a distinguished lecturer and author, his most significant work being a seven-volume history of civilization. Although 98 years old at the time of his death, his personality and general physical appearance were those of a person not over 50, so well-preserved was he in health and physical form.

He is said to have been one of the really great youthful men of his generation. During the first thirteen years of his live, Brown was an invalid, confined to a bed with nurses around the clock. One day, however, his nurse had to leave

3. Brown Landone, MD; https://brownlandone.wwwhubs.com/; accessed January 12, 2024.

to get more of his medicine. While she was gone, the house caught fire.

Brown smelled the smoke and remembered his father mentioning a very important chest upstairs, with valuable papers in it. With that in mind, the young boy climbed the stairs and retrieved the chest.

When he realized what he had done, Brown decided never to return to bed again except to sleep--and he never did.

Hundreds of similar experiences are known to science. In the presence of danger, superhuman strength is available. What's the source of this vast reserve of power and immediate wisdom? Insofar as present day knowledge is concerned, its sources in the largely unexplored field of subconscious motivation. Think of how we can change our lives by consciously using more of this strength we have within us.

And remember, you are as young as your faith, as old as your doubt, as young as your self-confidence, as old as your fear, as young as your hope, and as old as your despair. As long as you receive into yourself beauty, hope, cheer, courage, grandeur, and power from the infinite, you are young and able!

Superhuman strength is available through a vast reserve of power and immediate wisdom in the largely unexplored field of subconscious motivation.

Self-Confidence Versus Self-Doubt Study Questions

1. Millions of people have been and continue to be fascinated with comic book superheroes,—from Superman to Catwoman to Spider-Man to Wonder Woman, and even Teenage Mutant Ninja Turtles. How farfetched is it to consider each human being has such powers within themselves and are available to us?

2. Which superhero do you most identify with? Does this hero exhibit self-confidence? A positive attitude? Self-assurance? Composure? An action-packed personality? What can you learn from studying this hero's character?

3. What is the first action you would take if you could right now exhibit the superhuman strength within you?

Notes:

_____

_____

_____

_____

_____

_____

_____

_____

DISCOVER YOURSELF

"...the great man is he who in the midst of the crowd keeps with perfect sweetness the independence of solitude."

I've been pretty serious the past few days talking about a lot of things you don't hear about much, and I believe it's good for you to consider the creative power within your conscious and subconscious mind as well as the super-human strength within you. Recently, I read Emerson's essay on self-reliance all the way through again, and when I put it down, I thought how wonderful it would be if every person old enough to have any sense read that essay. It would still be the greatest commencement address in the world, something young people could really hang their hats on.

To this some will say, "Well, that's old stuff. It was written back in the 1840s." Newton invented differential calculus in 1665 and gave us the law of gravity in 1687. Should we

The independent thinker has all but disappeared from the face of the Earth.

toss those out the window? No, Emerson's *Self-Reliance*[4] is needed now even more than it was needed a hundred years ago because *never before have we had so many people following other people who don't know any more than they do.* It's getting so that no one will do anything anymore without asking permission or asking someone else's opinion of their plans. "What will people think?" has become the slogan of our times. The independent thinker, the independent actor, has all but disappeared from the face of the Earth.

In *Self-Reliance*, Emerson wrote, "Who so would be a man must be a non-conformist." By this he didn't mean

---

4. Excellent excerpts of *Self-Reliance* are found at the following website. Emerson's entire essay may be found at various sources: https://nationalhumanitiescenter.org/pds/triumphnationalism/cman/text8/selfreliance.pdf; accessed January 13, 2024.

breaking the law or becoming an iconoclast or a weirdo just to get attention. Just the opposite. He meant each of us should live according to our own individual nature, that each of us should seek the truth within ourselves and not blindly accept the beliefs bleated sheep-like by the crowd.

The crowd could be wrong, and in fact, it generally is. In another section Emerson wrote:

> What I must do is all that concerns me, not what the people think. This rule equally arduous in actual and an intellectual life may serve for the whole distinction between greatness and meanness. It is the harder because you'll always find those who think they know what is your duty better than you know it. It's easy in the world to live after the world's opinion. It's easy in solitude to live after our own, but the great man is he who in the midst of the crowd keeps with perfect sweetness the independence of solitude.

Self-Confidence Versus Self-Doubt Study Questions

1. Do you as a matter of routine dismiss anything other than current trends and waves of thought?

2. Would you seriously consider researching great independent thinkers of the past—such as Jesus of Nazareth, Albert Einstein, Benjamin Franklin, Nikola Tesla, Galileo Galilei, Aristotle, Ludwig van Beethoven, Michelangelo, Pascal, Hippocrates, Edwin Hubble, Johan Sebastian Bach, Marcus Aurelius, Mark Twain, Johannes Gutenberg—and reading some of their writings?

3. Fascinating women who have shaped history include Harriet Tubman, Catherine Booth, Fanny Crosby, Amy Carmichael, Rosa Parks, Susan B. Anthony, Corrie Ten Boom, Mother Teresa, Susanna Wesley, and Sojourner Truth.

4. I challenge you to choose two of the people listed and take time to read some of their thoughts in writing this week. Then, perhaps two more next week, and so on. You may be very surprised at what they have to say to you today about self-confidence.

Notes:

_____

_____

_____

_____

_____

_____

_____

_____

_____

_____

_____

_____

_____

_____

_____

_____

_____

_____

_____

_____

_____

_____

_____

MAKE UP YOUR MIND

*"Know thyself" are still two of the
most important words to live by.*

I wonder how many young people graduating from our schools today realize that their greatest chance for success as individuals is to make up their minds, to become individuals and not lose themselves in senseless emulation of the crowd. They should face the fact that all knowledge we now have is nothing, not even a grain of sand on the beach, compared to the truth and knowledge yet waiting for us. They—and we—should ask themselves, "What do I personally want to do and become as an individual?"

And if we find no quick and easy answer, we must learn to look for it and listen for it and meanwhile dedicate ourselves to look for truth in everything we do. Sooner or later to the person who wants to be an individual, the answer will come, and you will find the right direction. You will know peace and the quiet joy that comes only when you know that you are doing what you are were meant to do to bring you the kind of life you were meant to live.

Know thyself are still two of the most important words to live by. Knowing yourself includes knowing that the lack of confidence can stem from an inferiority complex, which is based on a false premise—comparing ourselves to other people. This is something we should never do since no two human beings are alike.

The well-adjusted, self-confident person isn't bothered because they can't do something as well as someone else. as well as someone else. for any one human being to be as good at everything as all other human beings.

Your greatest chance for success is to become an individual and not lose yourself in senseless imitation of the crowd.

Self-Confidence Versus Self-Doubt Study Questions

1. Have you made up your mind to the question, "What do I personally want to do and become as an individual?"

2. Do you suffer from an inferiority complex based on a false premise by comparing yourself to other people?

3. Did anyone come to mind when reading about comparing yourself to others? If yes, write a few traits or skills they have that you don't. Then write a few traits or skills that you have and they don't. Do you realize how futile it is to make comparisons?

Notes:

_____

_____

_____

_____

_____

_____

_____

_____

_____

_____

_____

_____

_____

_____

_____

_____

_____

_____

_____

_____

_____

_____

_____

_____

_____

_____

_____

_____

_____

_____

_____

_____

YOUR UNIQUENESS

When you understand fully and completely, intellectually and emotionally, that you are unique and different, you can't have an inferiority complex.

You are simply and perfectly you. You, as a personality, are not in competition with any other personality because there's not another person on the face of the Earth. You are an individual. You are unique. You're not supposed to be like any other person, and no other person is supposed to be like you.

We all can make ourselves feel inferior if we don't realize that we are unlike any other human being who ever lived on Earth. When we understand fully and completely, intellectually and emotionally, that we are unique and different, we *cannot* have an inferiority complex. How could we, since there's no standard against which to judge; every person is different. And, nothing on Earth happens purely by accident.

Each person is living because we were meant to live. Each of us has talents and abilities that are totally our own, unique to each of us. Your job, then, as a distinctive individual, is to learn to know yourself. If you do, you'll like yourself and build self-confidence. You will discover that you are quite a great person after all. You will recognize and accept what you can't do as well as some other people, but you will also understand and appreciate what you *can* do very well.

You are quite a great person after all!

"Confidence breeds confidence and negativity breeds negativity. Treat those around you with respect and dignity and they will thrive," said Sir Richard Branson, now estimated to be worth $5 billion. Branson is the epitome of someone who exudes self-confidence, despite many twists and turns during his life. He was a high school dropout and entered into his first successful business venture as a teenager with the magazine *Student*. When the magazine began losing money in the late 1960s, he formed Virgin Mail Order Records (so named because Branson considered himself inexperienced in business) to raise funds, and, in 1971, he opened the first British discount record store. In

1973, he helped form Virgin Records. In 1984, he became the majority backer of the airline that he renamed Virgin Atlantic Airways. Beginning with a single aircraft, the carrier succeeded despite fierce opposition from established airlines, and in 1992, Branson sold Virgin Records,"[5] for $1 billion. Today, the Virgin Group controls more than 400 companies in various fields of enterprise.

Speaking at the Virgin Hotel in Dallas, Texas, in 2024, Branson said, "There's a lot of people who have great ideas to start companies and they'll be told, 'No, that's already been thought of before, or that's not going to work,' so most of them will decide not to do it. But my attitude is that the best way of learning how to run a company is just to try it. Try to make sure you don't bankrupt your family in the process, but put your toe in the water within your means. Try again until you succeed."[6]

5. Erik Gregersen, "Richard Branson, British Entrepreneur," *Britannica;* https://www.britannica.com/biography/Richard-Branson; accessed January 14, 2024.

6. Irving Mejia-Hilario, "Billionaire Richard Branson and Virgin Hotels relaunch entrepreneur program," *Dallas Morning News,* January 10, 2024.

Self-Confidence Versus Self-Doubt Study Questions

1. Sir Richard Branson has been quoted numerous times over the years, and many quotes refer to self-confidence and the uniqueness of each individual. What do you think you could learn from reading his biography and quotes?

2. Have you had a business idea or an improvement suggestion concerning your current employment position? Why haven't you taken action on that idea or suggestion?

3. Do you understand fully and completely, intellectually and emotionally, that you are unique and different, with skills and talents that the world needs?

Notes:

_____

_____

_____

_____

_____

_____

_____

_____

FREEDOM TO BE

*"The secret of happiness is freedom
and the secret of freedom, courage."*

Pericles was one of the great Greek philosophers. He died of the plague in the year 429 BC, but achieved for himself permanent immortality by the things he did and said during his lifetime. How would you like to say something, just a few words, that people would still be repeating and talking about two centuries later? One of Pericles's quotations that has lived on and will never die: is, "Make up your minds, that happiness depends on being free, and freedom depends on being courageous."[7]

We are surrounded by truth—greatness comes from being able to see it. "The secret of happiness is freedom and the secret of freedom, courage." The more you think about those words, the more inspiring they become. If you

---

7.   Pericles's funeral oration was a speech written by Thucydides and delivered by Pericles for his history of the Peloponnesian War. Pericles delivered the oration not only to bury the dead but to praise democracy. https://www .thoughtco.com/pericles-funeral-oration-thucydides-version-111998; accessed January 15, 2024.

Human beings can't be happy without freedom.

write that and place it somewhere you can see it every morning and take it to heart, you can live the kind of a life you and your family would be proud of. You'll be as successful as a human being can be—and as happy. Human beings can't be happy without freedom.

People want the freedom to:

- Think their own thoughts and say what they think
- Choose their work and place of residence
- Move around when they feel like it
- Worship or not worship as they like
- Vote for whomever they please and speak out against anything they consider tyranny

Self-Confidence Versus Self-Doubt Study Questions

1. "The secret of happiness is freedom and the secret of freedom, courage." How would you rewrite that quotation to fit your right-now thinking about happiness, freedom, and courage?

2. Of the five "freedoms to" listed, which one is the most important to you? Why?

3. Of the five "freedoms to" listed, which one is the least important to you? Why?

Notes:

_____

_____

_____

_____

_____

_____

_____

_____

_____

_____

_____

_____

COURAGE AND MOTIVATION

Self-doubt, hesitation, and confusion often stem from the lack of a clear and worthy purpose. Get your purpose right and everything else will fall into place. There is always life for the living.

I remember what a terrific charge I got when Howard Hughes was being questioned by a committee in Washington. In front of the eyes of the whole world, when they began to badger him, he just stood up and told them exactly what he thought of them, and in no uncertain terms. And because of our great country, he could walk out of the hearings a free man. They couldn't stand him up against a wall and shoot him. They couldn't send him to some remote exile. All they could do was get red in the face and realize that maybe they had overstepped and were talking to a man who valued freedom and had the courage to keep it.

I believe freedom takes courage and lots of it to keep it. And while I don't presume to be improving on a quotation 2,000 years old, if Pericles's quotation were carried one more step, it might say, "And the secret of courage is knowledge." To be free and stay free, you have to have the knowledge of what it's all about, and that government, particularly our government, was designed to be the servant of the people, our paid servant, to keep alive our single most valuable commodity—our freedom.

Self-doubt, hesitation, and confusion often stem from the lack of a clear and worthy purpose.

First of all, you need to know what you believe in. It takes courage to stand up for your beliefs. Too many people doubt their own capacity for judgment, for knowing what's right or wrong. They wait to see what others do or say before they express an opinion of their own. So what do you believe in? What you believe in is what will happen to you. For belief is faith, and faith is still the greatest power on Earth.

A man might drag himself out of bed, grumbling, sleepy-eyed, and miserable at seven o'clock on Monday morning to go to work. But the same man at the same time in the morning on Saturday, as he gets up to play golf with his foursome, is wide-eyed, alert, and whistling as he makes his coffee and peers out the window to check the weather. Or maybe it's a shopping trip or the beginning of a family vacation. Whatever it may be, our reaction in any given situation depends on the cause and how it affects us.

Next, examine the way you approach your days. How you spend your days depends on your motivation. If you are focused on nothing more than quitting time, you will be operating on only the smallest fraction of your potential. The bigger and better the target you're shooting for, the more of yourself you'll use. And the more you fulfill yourself as a person, the happier, more free, more successful, and more contented you are.

Self-Confidence Versus Self-Doubt Study Questions

1.   What are you working toward? Is it worthy of your special powers? Does it call forth the best in you every day?

2.   Is your goal a great and constant vision before your eyes? If so, wonderful. If not, give it some thought. Nothing can bring you peace but you.

3.   This world belongs to the energetic. There is always a way to get what is desired. What is it you want? What is your motivation?

Notes:

_____

_____

_____

_____

_____

_____

_____

_____

_____

_____

_____

_____

DAY 29

HAPPINESS AND ACCOMPLISHMENT

The happiest people have always been those who fought the hard, clean fight and wound up on top of the pile. This is happiness that comes from accomplishment.

The way the world works is mind-boggling when thinking about it in the broadest terms. Millions of people dutifully plugging all the holes so that the vast machine starts on time and ends on time, and everything gets done.

The little boy is taken to the barber for his first haircut in a small town in eastern Oregon. A businessman puts his shoes to be shined in the plastic bag provided and hangs the bag on his hotel doorknob in Irving, Texas. The boy gets his first haircut, and the shoes are nicely shined when taken from the plastic bag next morning. Everything works to perfection, with everyone in place to do what needs to be done. It's astonishing and miraculous and wonderful.

Consider the teeming millions in New York City, who live and breathe and eat every day and sleep every night. The police keep the peace. The subways keep moving, the taxis too. The offices high above the street noise with deep carpeting are properly peopled also. The mail's delivered. And at the same time every day, in Key West, Florida, the charter captain readies his sport fishing tours for the day.

Life is astonishing and miraculous and wonderful.

There are human hands performing every job that needs performing. The president's breakfast of orange juice, poached eggs and toast will be prepared and served. A cracked sewer line will be repaired in Compton, California. While in the chilled operating room of Stanford University Hospital 400 miles north, a defective heart valve is being replaced in a patient who would die without it.

They're doing their jobs quite satisfactorily and taking home a paycheck. Something tells them that it's all worth the effort. That there's a reason for living out their lives. When these people die, no one exactly like them will ever again appear on the planet Earth. They will have served and

have been served by the rest. It's the most interesting phe-
nomenon. It's good to be part of it.

It's especially good to direct our lives to make excellent use of the options and aptitudes we received as our
share. To live as fully as we want to live and experience as
much of life as we choose to experience—and in doing so
make whatever contribution we can make for the benefit
of others.

Self-Confidence Versus Self-Doubt Study Questions

1. Do you agree that "the happiest people on Earth have always been the ones who have fought the hard, clean fight and have finally wound up on top of the pile. This is the happiness that comes from accomplishment"?

2. Francis Bacon said, "Wise men *make* more opportunities than they *find*." Are you willing to look with new eyes and perspective and realize that there is no limit to what you can accomplish other than the limits you impose upon yourself?

3. Stop for a few moments and think about all the activities going on around you—whether you're sitting at home, at the office, in a coffee shop, or wherever. Think about how people are serving and being served in some way for the benefit of others. Are you doing your share?

Notes:

_____

_____

_____

_____

_____

_____

_____
_____
_____
_____
_____
_____
_____
_____
_____
_____
_____
_____
_____
_____
_____
_____
_____
_____
_____
_____
_____
_____
_____
_____
_____
_____

OPPORTUNITY KNOCKS

Opportunity's knuckles are bleeding and raw to the bone from knocking every day of your life. You just have to see it!

Don't ever believe the saying that "opportunity knocks only once." Opportunity's knuckles are bleeding and raw to the bone from knocking every day of your life. You just have to be able to see it.

The myth that we only have one big break in life causes a lot of worry. If one opportunity escapes or fails, there will be another one. The *fear* surrounding opportunity holds good people back from doing great things as we learn to *doubt* ourselves.

Famed Dr. Charles Mayo is quoted as saying, "Worry affects the circulation, the heart, the glands, the whole nervous system." And he goes on to say, "I have never known anyone who died from overwork, but many who have died from doubt."

Find ways to improve and upgrade your life while life is humming along at its best. Don't wait until you've lost a job to start thinking about possible alternatives. Think about options when all is going well and you're under no pressure nor suffering from a loss of self-esteem.

Gordon Graham wrote, "There are two kinds of discontent in this world. The discontent that works and the discontent that wrings its hands. The first gets what it wants, and the second loses what it had. There is no cure for the first but success, and no cure at all for the second."

Discontent has been called divine by many who understand that *discontent drives opportunity*. At one time or another, we're all looking for better ways to find comfort, a better and faster device with more storage, or a better tasting cup of coffee.

Ideas can provide us with autonomy and self-confidence—if we don't doubt. Ideas can give us freedom. Good ideas are wondrous and delightful, a boost within. Opening the door to opportunities when they knock explains why those people have accumulated vastly greater incomes after retirement than they ever did on the job they so diligently worked for many years. That can be you!

Fear surrounding opportunity holds good people back from doing great things.

Self-Confidence Versus Self-Doubt Study Questions

1. Start a list, and at the top, write, "I need better, more interesting, more rewarding work." Under that, you might first ask the question, "Is it to be found with my current company? Business? What can I do now to make a more important contribution than the work I'm presently doing?" Another question to write might be, "What would I rather do for a living than anything else in the world?"

   As you doodle with such ideas, more ideas will come. Now you're using what you were born to use and putting to work our most valuable possessions— thinking with your conscious and subconscious.

2. Write page after page, as long as the ideas pour out. Don't stop when you get your first exciting idea. Write it down, by all means underscored. Draw a star beside it or a circle around it. Then press on for new and better ideas, which will come. Later you can number each in order of importance.

3. After each idea, ask, "Am I prepared to handle such work? What would it take to prepare me for such work?" Another excellent question to write down is, "What can I do that will best serve the people of my community, state, country, or even the whole world?"

Notes:

_____

_____

_____

_____

_____

_____

_____

_____

_____

_____

_____

_____

_____

_____

_____

_____

_____

_____

_____

_____

_____

_____

_____

_____

_____

_____

_____

_____

_____

_____

_____

_____

_____

_____

_____

_____

_____

_____

CONCLUSION

Self-confidence produces numerous ideas for improvement. Becoming more aware of what people want brings you closer to the next big thing. In conclusion, let's look specifically at starting your own business.

Opportunities are all around, but before you go into a business of your own, you need to apply a few rules:

- One, is the business really needed?

- Two, is it a business with which you are intimately familiar?

- Three, is it a business you will enjoy devoting many years to developing?

- Four, do you have sufficient capital to operate at a loss for a couple of years if necessary?

Of course, there are exceptions to every rule, including these four. For example, there are thousands of successful businesses that are not really needed. Look at the diamond industry worth millions. No one *needs* a diamond, but enough people want to own or gift a diamond to make it a very successful industry.

There's one big exception when it comes to having a successful business of your own—are you especially good at something you love to do? If so, it can usually turn into a successful business.

It could be anything from interior decorating to landscaping to teaching art to car repair. Perhaps the best rule of all is to pick a business that is already well established, a business that supplies something people are already using or needing—then go into your business and do it better.

Pick a business you really enjoy and then do it better than the other ninety-five percent.

Keep in mind that about ninety-five percent of people in any given line of business are doing just enough to get by. Pick a business you really enjoy and then get in the top five

Your profits
will always be
in direct proportion
to the number of
people you can serve
multiplied by the unit
of profit on each sale.

percent by doing it better than ninety-five percent of those people. In this way, you'll always succeed. It's only a matter of time, and time is vital.

Dun & Bradstreet doesn't consider a business a success until it has been operating for at least five years. So figure on five years to get over the initial hump; and remember that your profits will always be in direct proportion to the number of people you can serve multiplied by the unit of profit on each sale.

That is an important fact to remember, and most people going into business for themselves forget it. This last part is vital and should be figured as closely as possible before you go into this business that has been running around in the back of your mind.

If you want an overall rule that applies to your success in any line of work, remember this: your rewards in life will always be in exact proportion to your contribution. If you seek more in the way of rewards, devise means of increasing your contribution.

Only a few people know at an early age what career they want to pursue—the rest of us have to find out by trying on this hat and then another. And that's good. In today's world, there are so many interesting opportunities. It's quite difficult for most people to make a perfect decision the first time.

Perfect or not, it seems that most people largely look at their work as permanent, something they are stuck in, like it or not. If the career track is not what was expected, people often think that's just too bad. This is especially true of people lacking self-confidence.

The young person who dreams of being an oceanographer or expert on pollution winds up being a lawyer or a CPA. Be that as it may, the person who dreams of more interesting, more challenging, and perhaps more rewarding work should ask quite seriously, "What is preventing me from fulfilling my dream?"

No matter what field you choose, there are always good reasons to take advantage of ideas and opportunities that present. If you can think of the field you would like very much to enter, chances are you can if you're willing to make a few sacrifices.

It might mean going back to school or starting all over at the bottom, but if you want it enough, you can make it happen. Opportunities are everywhere—from A to Z, from aviation to zippers. There's a kind of work that can be congenial and interesting for just about anyone if you go to the trouble of discovering what it is and then qualifying for it.

The most fortunate people on Earth are those who enjoy and can find personal fulfillment and satisfaction in their work—which takes self-confidence minus doubt. That's you!

ABOUT EARL NIGHTINGALE

Earl Nightingale (1921-1989) was a man of many talents and interests—nationally syndicated radio personality, entrepreneur, philosopher, US Marine, and more. One thread united all his pursuits—a passion for excellence and living a meaningful existence.

Earl Nightingale's life began simply. He grew up in Long Beach, California. His parents had little money, and his father disappeared when he was twelve. But even as a boy, Earl was always asking questions, always reading in his local public library, wanting to understand the way life works.

Stationed aboard the battleship USS Arizona, Earl Nightingale was one of a handful of survivors when that ship was destroyed and sank at Pearl Harbor. After being separated from the Marine Corps, and starting with practically nothing, in ten years he founded and headed four corporations. He wrote, sold, and produced fifteen radio and television programs per week.

Nightingale appeared on all major networks and for four years was the star of the dramatic series *Sky King,* which was carried on more than 500 stations of the Mutual Radio Network. He also began an insurance agency and in twelve months led it from last to sixth place in the nation with one of the world's largest companies.

The Nation's Press carried the astounding story of the phenomenally successful young man who, at thirty-five had become financially independent. He produced his famous recording of *The Strangest Secret,* revealing how anyone can make the most of their capabilities and attain a rich, full measure of success and happiness, right in their present job or position. Its theme is: "How to achieve greater success and enjoy greater happiness and peace of mind."

This inspiring recording broke sales records at the time, selling in the multimillions to major industries, retailers and salespeople, clubs and associations, parents, students, and people in virtually all walks of life. His masterful record-ing has been adapted into a book and videos.

THANK YOU FOR READING THIS BOOK!

If you found any of the information helpful, please take a few minutes and leave a review on the bookselling platform of your choice.

BONUS GIFT!

Don't forget to sign up to try our newsletter and grab your free personal development ebook here:

soundwisdom.com/classics